Knitting

Learn to knit six great projects

By Anne Akers Johnson

KLUTZ® is a kids' company staffed entirely by real human beings. For those of you who collect corporate mission statements, here's ours:

Create wonderful things
Be good • Have fun

WRITE US

We would love to hear your comments regarding this or any of our books. We have many!

KLUTZ®

455 Portage Avenue
Palo Alto, CA 94306

Book printed in China.
Knitting needles manufactured in Korea.
Yarn manufactured in China.
All other parts manufactured in Taiwan.

Distributed in the UK by
Scholastic UK Ltd.,
Westfield Road, Southam
Warwickshire, England, CV47 0RA

ISBN 1-57054-861-7
4 1 5 8 5 7 0 8

VISIT OUR WEBSITE

You can check out all the stuff we make, find a nearby retailer, sign up for a newsletter, e-mail us, or just goof off.

KLUTZ.com
Come on in!

Basics

8   first things first
14 casting on
18 knitting
20 purling

22 casting off
26 nitty-gritty details
38 finishing

Projects

42 pocket purse

50 skinny scarf

62 purse

72 cell phone sock

56 sunglass bag

82 hat

Basics

In this section you'll learn everything you need to know to start knitting. Unless you already know how to knit, this is the place to start.

what comes with this book

This book comes with everything
you need to start knitting.

WORSTED WEIGHT YARN
This yarn works for all the
projects in this book.

KNITTING NEEDLES
We've provided size 8 needles:
the right size for all the
projects in the book.

BUTTONS
The cell sock and the pocket purse
both need a button. These buttons
will work for either project.

A CROCHET HOOK

The crochet hook is used to fix mistakes (just in case you make any), and to do a little crochet for the hat. If you lose it, you can buy another size F hook at a yarn or craft store.

YARN NEEDLE

You'll need this to sew the seams on your projects.

RULER

We've printed a ruler on the inside front cover. Use it to measure your projects.

A few things you'll need to round up:

SCISSORS, A NEEDLE & THREAD

You'll need these to sew the buttons onto the pocket purse and the cell sock.

winding your yarn into a ball

The yarn that comes with this book is wrapped into skeins. Whenever your yarn comes this way, you'll need to roll it into a ball before you use it. If you try to knit from the skein, your yarn will tangle into a big mess.

1

A skein of yarn looks like this:

Gently pull the skein apart, and you'll see it's a big loop. Usually it will be tied to keep it neat. Untie or cut the yarn that is tied around the loop and find the end.

Untie or cut this loop.

3

Hold the end of the yarn with your thumb and wrap the yarn around two fingers.

4

Then take the yarn off your fingers and wind the yarn around it as shown:

If it's hard to pull the yarn off your fingers, you're winding it too tightly. Loosen up!

② Ask a friend to hold the yarn for you...

...or drape the yarn over the back of a chair so it doesn't tangle as you wind

⑤ Wind the yarn maybe five or six times...

⑥ ...then turn the ball of yarn and make a few more wraps in a different direction. Continue to wind the yarn every which way to make a more-or-less round ball.

When you buy your yarn at a yarn store, it's worth asking if they'll wind it into a ball for you. Many stores will do this with no charge.

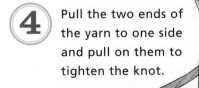

tying a slip knot

Every knitting project begins with a slip knot, so
make sure you know how to tie one before you go on.

long end

1 Start by making a loop in
your yarn where you want
the knot to be. Make sure
the long end passes over
the short end.

2 Next, fold the loop over
so it crosses the
short end...

3 ...and pick up the short
end with your knitting
needle like so:

4 Pull the two ends of
the yarn to one side
and pull on them to
tighten the knot.

Your slip knot should be loose enough that you can easily fit two knitting needles through it.

5 Then pull on the short end until the knot just rests against the knitting needle.

the easiest way to hold your hands

There's only one rule about how to hold your hands while you knit: If it works, it's right. Still, if you find yourself struggling to hold your needles, the yarn, *and* learn to knit all at the same time, this page will help. These instructions may be a little confusing if you haven't actually tried to knit yet, so it's OK to skip this page for now. If you need a little help once you get started, it's right here.

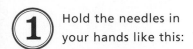

1 Hold the needles in your hands like this:

2 Pinch both needles together with your left hand while you wrap the yarn with your right.

You can hold the needles the same whether you're casting on, knitting, purling or casting off.

If you watch other people knit, you'll see that there are lots of different ways to hold your hands. You'll find another way on page 24. Once you feel pretty comfortable knitting, go ahead and give the second method a try. It might help you knit a little faster.

practice makes perfect
(perfect enough, anyway)

The best way to learn to knit is to **make a practice piece first.** That way if you make mistakes or your stitches are uneven to start, **it just doesn't matter**. When you're finished with the practice piece you can unravel it and use the yarn to make one of the great projects in this book.

Look for the practice piece instructions at the end of the pages on knitting, purling and casting off. Follow these directions as you work through each section and you'll have a chance to practice everthing you're learning.

(3) Then return the needle to your right hand while you finish your knit stitch. Or your cast-on or purl stitch. **Easy**.

Finally. You're ready to get started.

casting on

Before you can start knitting, you have to tie on the first row of stitches. This is called *casting on*. There are lots of different ways to cast on. The method on this page is one of the easiest to learn, but you have to be very careful not to make your knots too tight. If you do, you'll have a hard time knitting your first row.

You'll find another method of casting on on page 18. Try both and use whichever method works best for you.

1

Start by tying a slip knot around one needle. The loop should be loose enough that you can easily slide your second needle into it. Which is what you'll do next.

long end

Leave a tail of about 6 inches.

4

...and pull it down between the two needles like so:

7

Pull the needles apart slightly. There will be a loop on each of them.
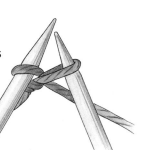

8

Transfer the loop on the right needle to the left needle...

9

...then remove the right needle so both stitches are on the left needle.

2

Poke the right needle **up** through the first loop on the left needle. Make sure the right needle is **behind** the left one.

 3

Now wrap the long piece of yarn behind and around the right needle...

Make sure you wrap the long end of yarn, not the short one.

 5

Slide the right needle down, using it to catch the yarn between the two needles...

6

...then pull it down through the first loop as shown.

 10

Repeat steps 2–9, always working with the stitch closest to the tip of the left needle, until you've cast on as many stitches as you need.

Practice casting on until you can do it without looking at the instructions.

Keep it loose! Each loop should be loose enough to fit around two needles at the same time.

15

casting on with one needle

This is another way of casting on. It's a little tricky to learn but, once you've got it, it's easy and fast. It's a good method to try if your stitches are always too tight when you cast on with two needles.

1 Instead of tying a slip knot at the end of your yarn, you have to tie it somewhere in the middle. To figure out exactly where, allow about an inch for every stitch you want plus about 6 inches for a tail. So to cast on 20 stitches, tie your knot 26 inches from the end.

3 Without moving your thumb and first finger, close your hand around both strands of yarn, and pull the needle down between them. Look at the next picture to be sure you've got it right.

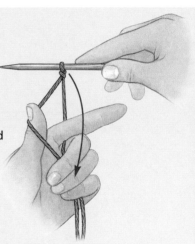

6 ...like so:

7 Now let the loop drop off your thumb...

8 ...and use your thumb to pull the new loop on your needle snug (but not tight).

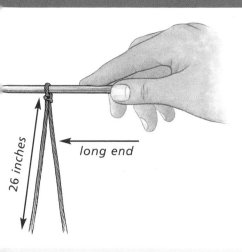

26 inches ← long end

2 Poke your left thumb and first finger in-between the two ends of yarn, letting the yarn run over your other fingers exactly as shown.

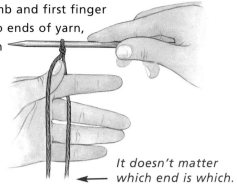

It doesn't matter which end is which.

4 You'll have a loop of yarn on your thumb and on your first finger.

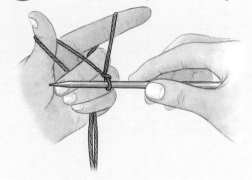

5 Poke your needle **up** through the loop on the left thumb...

...and pick up the yarn that runs in front of your first finger (we've marked it in red). Pull this piece of yarn right back through the thumb loop...

9 When you're finished, you'll have two loops on your needle and will be ready to add another. Repeat steps 5-8 until you've cast on as many stitches as you like.

Keep your stitches about 1/4 inch apart and remember: Don't pull the knots too tight!

LEFTIES: *You might find it easier to hold the yarn in your right hand.*

17

knitting

Once you've cast on, you're ready to start knitting. *Finally.*

1 Since you're making the practice piece, start by casting on 20 stitches.

long end

In this picture we cast-on with two needles. If you cast on with one, both ends of yarn will be at the top.

← *short end*

3 Wrap the long end of the yarn around the right needle...

4 ... pull it down between the two needles...

5 ...then slide the right needle down and pull the new loop of yarn through the first one.

8 Repeat steps 2–6 until all the loops have been moved from the left needle to the right.

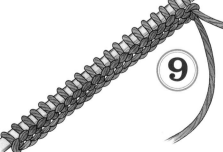

9 Turn the right needle over to make it the left needle. You're ready to work the next row.

2 Poke the right needle **up** through the first loop, making sure it goes **behind** the left needle.

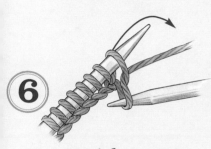

6 Turn the **right** needle so it points up, and pull the first loop all the way off the **left** needle.

The stitch you just pulled off.

7 You'll end up with one loop on the right needle and 19 on the left.

KNITTING FOR LEFTIES

You use both of your hands to knit, so this is one of the few times when being a lefty doesn't change anything. Follow these directions and you'll do just fine.

practice piece

1 Cast on 20 stitches.

Whenever the next stitch is to be knit, it will be colored purple.

2 Knit all the cast-on stitches.

3 Knit nine more rows, or as many as you need to get the hang of it. Your work will look like this:

You've just knit the garter stitch.

Garter stitch = knit every row

purling

Purling is just like knitting, except backwards.
Sort of.

1

To purl, poke your right needle through the **top** of the first loop on the left needle, making sure it passes **in front** of the left.

3

Pull this new loop **up** through the first loop on the left needle...

4

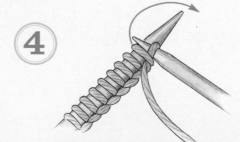

...then pull the first loop all the way off the left needle.

5

the stitch you just pulled off

You'll end up with one stitch on the right needle and the rest on the left.

Whenever the next stitch is a purl, it will be colored green.

2

Wrap the long end of the yarn around the right needle as shown.

4

Purl all the stitches in the next row.

5

Then **knit** all the stitches in the next row.

6

Repeat steps 4 and 5 until you've got the hang of it. End with a purl row. Your practice piece will look something like this:

You've just knit the stockinette stitch.

Stockinette stitch = knit one row, purl one row

6

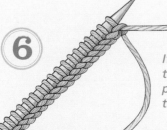

If you're making the practice piece, you'll knit the next row.

Repeat steps 1–4 until you've purled the whole row and all the stitches are on the right needle. Turn the needle over to make it the left needle.

casting off

When your project is finished you have to tie off the last row so it doesn't unravel. This is called **casting off**. If you can, cast off on a knit row.

1

Knit the first two stitches as always.

2

Use your **left** needle to pick up the first loop on the **right** needle...

5

You've just cast off your first stitch. There will be one loop left on the right needle.

Make sure your work looks like the picture.

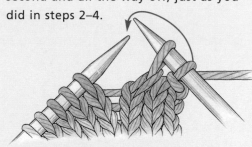

6

Knit another stitch, then lift the first loop on the **right** needle over the second and all the way off, just as you did in steps 2–4.

8

Use the needle to pull the yarn end all the way through the last loop.

9

Pull the end tight.

3

...pull it up **over** the second loop...

4

...and off the **right** needle. Let the loop drop off the **left** needle.

7

Repeat step 6 until there's just one loop left. It will be on the right needle. Cut the yarn so it's about 6 inches long.

6 inches

Sometimes you'll need to cast off a purled stitch. Once you've purled the stitch, cast off in exactly the same way you would a knit stitch.

practice piece continued

7

Cast off the next row.

8

If you want to unwind your work and use the yarn for something else, simply pull on the end of the yarn to unravel it. Wind the yarn back onto the ball. Your yarn will look a little kinky from being knit, but don't worry. The kinks will disappear as you knit your next project.

9

If you want to save your sample, cut the end short and pull it through the last stitch. Pull tight.

another way to hold your hands

This is another way of holding your needles and yarn while you knit. It helps you knit a little faster. **It's easier than it looks,** but wait until you're pretty comfortable knitting before you give it a try. If it doesn't work for you, **don't worry.** Go back to the method shown on page 12.

1 Wrap the yarn around your right pinky...

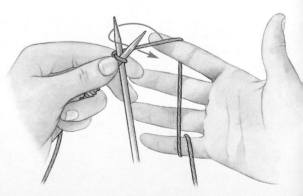

4 When you're ready to start knitting, pinch the needles together with your **left** hand and use your right index finger to loop the yarn around the needle. Look at the picture to be sure you've got it right.

2 ...then up **behind** and around your index finger.

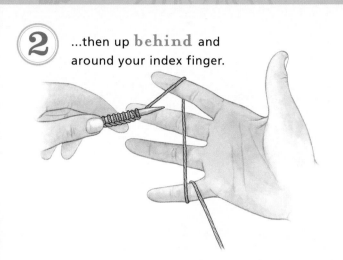

3 Now, without unwinding the yarn from your right hand, pick up the needles, holding one in each hand as shown.

5 Transfer the right needle back to your right hand and complete the stitch.

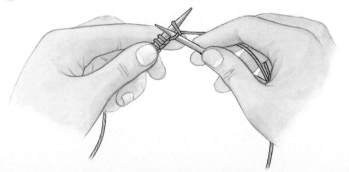

This technique works the same whether you're knitting or purling.

gauge

One of the trickiest things about learning to knit is getting the tension right. When you're still learning, it's easy to knit too tightly or too loosely. Luckily, there's an easy way make sure you've got it right. It's called **checking your gauge**.

Every yarn has a gauge. This is the number of stitches it takes to knit an inch. The yarn that comes with this book is called **worsted weight**, and has a gauge of 4-$\frac{1}{2}$ stitches per inch.

To be really accurate, it's best to **check your gauge over 4 inches**. If you're knitting 4-$\frac{1}{2}$ stitches per inch, that means that over 4 inches you'll have **18** stitches.

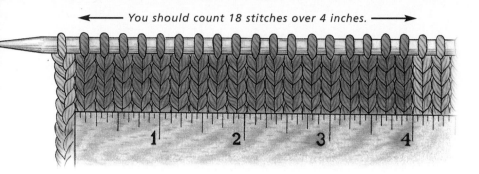
You should count 18 stitches over 4 inches.

1   2   3   4

If you count **more** than 18 stitches over 4 inches, you're knitting too tightly. **Try to knit a little looser.**

If you count **fewer** than 18 stitches over 4 inches, you're knitting too loosely. **Try to knit a little tighter.**

To check your gauge, lay your work out flat without stretching or scrunching it up. Lay a ruler on top of it. It's easier to count stitches if you measure in the middle of the work, not right from the edge, which can sometimes be a little uneven.

Gauge isn't that important for most of the projects in this book. It's not the end of the world if your scarf is 5-$\frac{1}{2}$ inches wide instead of 5 inches. Gauge is really important if you're knitting something like the hat (or a sweater) and you want it to fit right. Knit too tightly and your hat will be too small. Too loosely and it will be too big.

If you're making something where gauge really counts and you consistently knit too tightly, you can solve the problem by knitting with needles one size bigger. If you consistently knit too loosely, the next size smaller might solve the problem.

buying more yarn

We've provided enough yarn to make most of the projects in this book. Even so, once you start knitting, it won't be long before you start thinking about buying more yarn. Your first visit to a yarn store can be a little confusing. Very confusing even. Here are a few tips to make it easier:

TIP #1 **The most important thing you need to know when you buy more yarn is its gauge.** If you want to buy more yarn, look for something that's the same gauge as the yarn that comes with this book: 4-1/2 stitches per inch when knit on size 8 needles. It doesn't matter whether you buy yarn made of wool, acrylic, cotton or some blend. **It's all about the gauge.**

Usually a yarn's gauge is printed right on the label. Sometimes it will simply tell you the gauge and the needle size. **That's easy.** It's more common to see something like this:

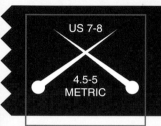
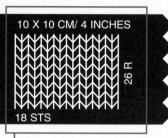

This just tells you the needle size to use. In this case either size 7 or 8 will give you a gauge of $4\frac{1}{2}$ to 5 stitches per inch.

This picture represents a piece of knitting, and tells you that 18 stitches will measure 4 inches. Because it's always best to measure your gauge over 4 inches instead of just one, yarn labels often give you the gauge this way. If you do the math, you'll know that 18 stitches over 4 inches is the same as $4\frac{1}{2}$ stitches per inch. **Perfect.**

The easiest way to buy yarn is to ask a salesperson for help. Which brings us to the second most important thing you need to know about going to the yarn store:

TIP #2 Knitters are nice people.

They love to help new knitters, so don't be afraid to ask for advice. Most stores organize their yarn by gauge, so the salesperson can probably point you to a whole pile of yarn that will work for your project. Even experienced knitters ask for help when they go to the store. **Really.**

And when you buy your yarn at a store that specializes in knitting, they'll often help you out with a project if you get stuck. **That's how nice knitters are.**

when you run out of yarn

If you're halfway through a project and you run out of yarn, **don't panic. It's easy to add more**. It's always better to run out of yarn at the end of a row, so keep your eyes on your yarn as you get close to the end. If you run out in the middle of a row, it's best just to unravel back to the start of a row (more about unraveling on page 35). Then follow the directions on this page.

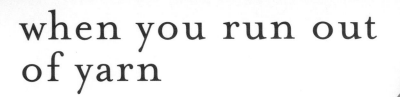

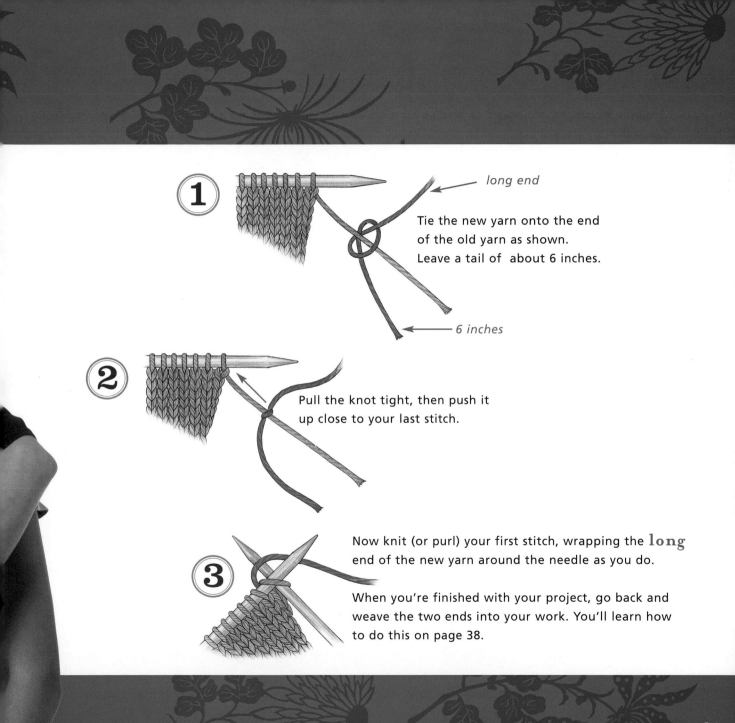

1 *long end*

Tie the new yarn onto the end of the old yarn as shown. Leave a tail of about 6 inches.

6 inches

2 Pull the knot tight, then push it up close to your last stitch.

3 Now knit (or purl) your first stitch, wrapping the **long** end of the new yarn around the needle as you do.

When you're finished with your project, go back and weave the two ends into your work. You'll learn how to do this on page 38.

picking up a dropped stitch

When you're still learning to knit, it's a good idea to stop and **count the stitches** on your needle every once in awhile. If you don't have as many as you're supposed to, you've probably dropped a stitch somewhere along the way. You can unravel your work until you get back to a place with the right number of stitches (see page 35), OR if the dropped stitch is just a few rows back, you can use your crochet hook to pick up the stitch and carry on. **Much easier**.

If you're knitting the **stockinette stitch...**

 ...a dropped stitch will look something like this:

You'll see a loop hanging out, and a little ladder of yarn leading up to the needles — one for every row the stitch has unraveled. **Yikes!**

If you drop a stitch while you're doing the garter stitch, it's best to simply unravel back to that spot. You'll learn how on page 35. Make sure you have the right number of stitches on your needle before you start knitting again.

If you notice the dropped stitch while you're on a purl row, don't worry. Just turn your work over to the front and fix it as shown on this page, then turn it over again and finish your purl row.

2 Poke your crochet hook up through the loose loop, pick up the lowest strand of yarn...

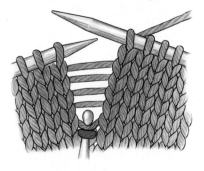

3 ...and pull it through the loop.

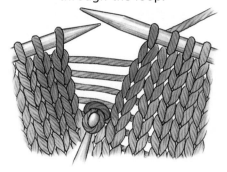

4 Pick up all the loose strands in the same way.

When you've picked up all the stitches, simply slip the loop off your crochet hook and onto the needle filled with to-be-knit stitches (the one without the yarn hanging off it). You're ready to knit again!

too many stitches

If you suddenly find yourself with **more** stitches than you started with, it's likely that you've doubled a stitch over somewhere. This only happens on the first stitch of a row.

right:

When you're knitting your first stitch, make sure the yarn is at the back of the needle as shown:

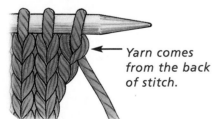

← Yarn comes from the back of stitch.

On a purl row the opposite is true. The yarn should be in front.

wrong:

If it's pulled over and in front of your needle, that first stitch will look like two stitches.

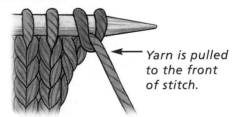

← Yarn is pulled to the front of stitch.

If you have more stitches on your needle than you started with, it's best to unravel until you get back to the right number of stitches.

unravelling

Every once in awhile, you'll make a mistake in your knitting, and there's nothing to do but unravel your work partway and knit it over again. Maybe you find yourself with more stitches than you started out with, or not nearly as many. Or maybe you dropped a stitch so far back that it would be hard to fix the usual way. Unravelling can be a little scary at first, but just work slowly and carefully and *you'll be fine*.

1 Slip the stitches off your needle, and pull on the end of yarn to unravel your stitches as far as you need to.

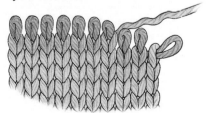

2 Then carefully put all the stitches back on your needle. Make sure to push the needle **towards** the side with the yarn hanging off.

Push the needle through the stitches from the back so they look just like this:

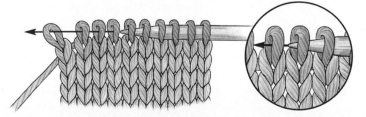

sewing seams

Except for the scarf, all the projects in this book require some simple sewing. There are a couple of different ways to do this. We show you the straight stitch and the whip stitch. Try them both and use whichever you like best. Before you get started, you're going to need to find the yarn needle that comes with this book.

1

No matter which stitch you plan to use, start by threading some yarn through your yarn needle, then pull the yarn almost all the way through both layers. Tie the ends together as shown.

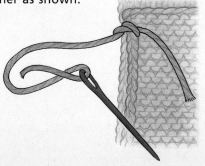

2 A straight stitch looks like this:

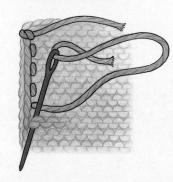

Sew close to the edge of your work.

A whip stitch looks like this:

It's always a good idea to pin the edges of your project together before you start sewing.

3 To finish either stitch, take one more stitch and push your needle though it to make a knot.

weaving your yarn in

At the end of every project, you'll have at least a couple of loose ends hanging off. Hide these ends by weaving them into your work.

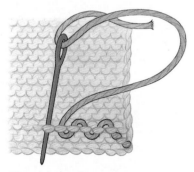

Thread the loose yarn onto your yarn needle and weave it through the stitches on the back of your work. Weave in at least 2 inches, then trim the yarn close to your work.

Always leave a tail of at least 6 inches, so you have plenty of yarn to weave in at the end.

blocking your work

What is blocking?

Blocking makes your project look more finished. It evens out lumpy stitches and gives you a chance to shape your work just right.

When to block:

You don't have to block things made of acrylic yarn (like the stuff that comes with this book). **Most of the projects in this book don't need to be blocked** even if you make them out of wool or some other natural fiber. But if you've knit something using a natural fiber and it isn't shaped quite right, or the stitches look lumpy, **give it a try**.

How to block:

There are a lot of different ways to block your work. **Here's an easy way** that works especially well for small projects.

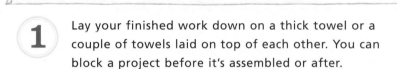

1–2 inches

1 Lay your finished work down on a thick towel or a couple of towels laid on top of each other. You can block a project before it's assembled or after.

2 Now hold a steaming iron about one to two inches away from your work and steam the whole thing. **Never** let the iron touch the yarn or you'll flatten your stitches.

3 Put the iron down and gently smooth your knitted piece to shape it. Give it another steam, then leave it to dry completely. It sometimes helps to pin your work to the towel after you've steamed it so that it holds its shape as it dries.

Projects

If you've successfully completed your practice piece, you're ready to start making one of the projects. You have enough yarn to make the first five projects in this book or the hat or the scarf. It's probably a good plan to start with the smaller projects first.

Pocket Purse

This pretty little purse is perfect for holding coins, keys or anything small you don't want to lose. It knits up quickly and easily, making it a good first project.

WHAT YOU NEED

SIZE 8 NEEDLES · 25 YARDS OF WORSTED WEIGHT YARN
A $\frac{3}{4}$-INCH BUTTON · YOUR YARN NEEDLE · NEEDLE AND THREAD

1 Cast on 15 stitches, leaving a tail of about 8 inches.

2 **Knit** all the stitches in the first row.

purple means knit
green means purl

3 **Purl** the next row.

4 Repeat steps 2 and 3 until your work measures 3 inches. It doesn't matter whether you end with a knit or a purl row.

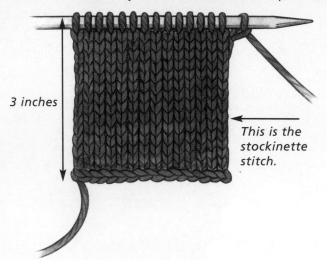

3 inches

This is the stockinette stitch.

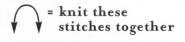 = knit these stitches together

knit together   knit together

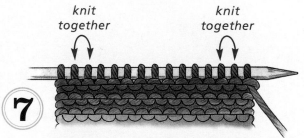

7 You're ready to shape the flap now. To do this:

knit 1 stitch • **knit** 2 stitches together
knit 9 stitches • **knit** 2 stitches together
knit 1 stitch

5 Now, **knit** every row...

8 You should end up with 13 stitches on your needle. The next row is almost the same, but there are fewer stitches in the middle:

knit 1 stitch • **knit** 2 stitches together
knit 7 stitches • **knit** 2 stitches together
knit 1 stitch

6 ...until your piece measures 8 inches.

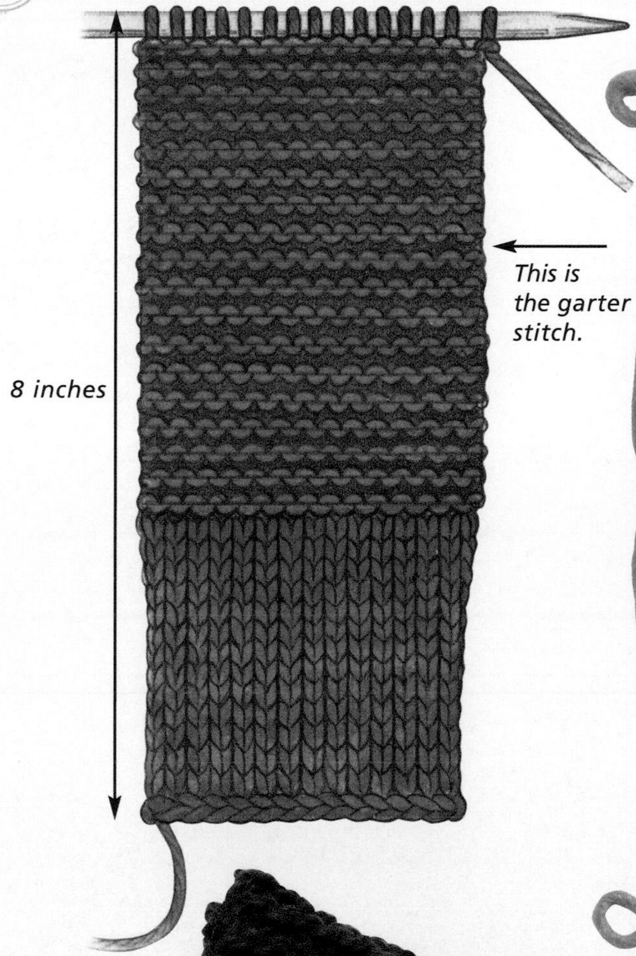

8 inches

This is the garter stitch.

↑↓ = **knit these stitches together**

Knitting two stitches together is called **decreasing** because it leaves you with fewer stitches than you started with and makes your work skinnier. Knitting two stitches together is easy, so don't let those little arrows intimidate you.

Here's how it's done:

1 Push your right needle through the two stitches to be knit together, and wrap the yarn around the needle as always.

2 Pull both stitches off the needle as you knit.

3 Your work will look like this:

45

knit together

9 There should be 11 stitches on your needle. You're going to make the button hole on this row. Here's how:
knit 1 stitch • **knit** 2 stitches together
knit 2 stitches

Next you're going to add a loop.

10 To do this, bring the yarn around to the front of the right needle...

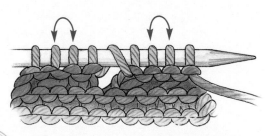

13 You should have nine stitches on your needle. One is the loop you added.
knit 1 • **knit** 2 stitches together
knit 3 stitches *(knit the new loop as if it were any other stitch)*
knit 2 stitches together • **knit** 1 stitch

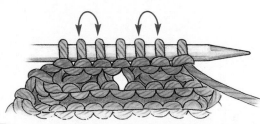

14 There will be seven stitches on your needle.
knit 1 • **knit** 2 stitches together
knit 1 stitch • **knit** 2 stitches together
knit 1 stitch

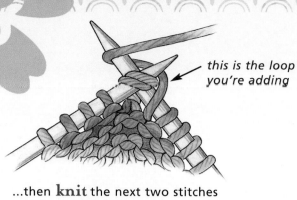

this is the loop you're adding

11 ...then **knit** the next two stitches together, wrapping the yarn around the right needle as always.

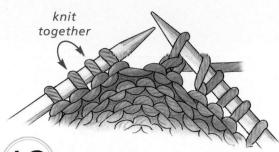

knit together

12 Finish out the row like this:
knit 1 stitch
knit 2 stitches together
knit 1 stitch

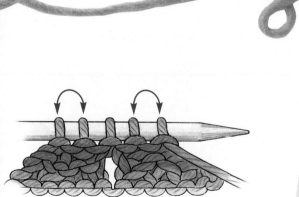

15 There will be five stitches on your needle.
knit 2 stitches together
knit 1 stitch
knit 2 stitches together

16 There will be three stitches on your needle. **Knit** all three stitches together...

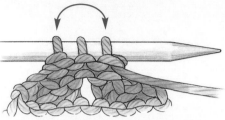

17 ...like so:

19 Thread the yarn through your plastic needle and weave the yarn into the back of the flap. Trim the end short.

The back will look like this at the bottom.

20 Center a button 1 inch from the bottom of the purse and sew it in place using a regular needle and thread. Look at the picture to make sure you've got it right.

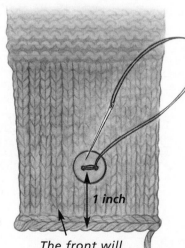

1 inch

The front will look like this at the bottom.

18 Cut the yarn so it's about 6 inches long, then remove the knitting needle and pull the end of the yarn through the loop. Pull this knot tight.

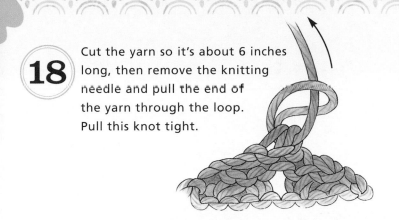

21

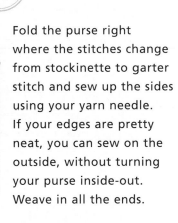

Fold the purse right where the stitches change from stockinette to garter stitch and sew up the sides using your yarn needle. If your edges are pretty neat, you can sew on the outside, without turning your purse inside-out. Weave in all the ends.

Skinny Scarf

This is probably the easiest project in the book, but it takes the longest to finish. You might want to shop for new yarn to make the scarf, as it will use up all of the yarn that comes with this book.

WHAT YOU NEED
SIZE 8 NEEDLES · ABOUT 200 YARDS OF WORSTED WEIGHT YARN

1 Cast on 20 stitches. **Knit** every row until the scarf is as long as you want it (5 feet is good).

2 Cast off and weave in the ends. It's that easy.

stripes

It's easy to add stripes to your scarf. In fact, if you've ever run out of yarn and had to add more, you already know how.

 When you're ready to change colors, cut the yarn end so it's about 6 inches long. Tie the new color onto the starting yarn and push it up close to the last stitch.

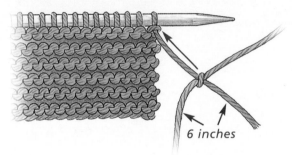

6 inches

 When you start knitting the next row, knit with the new color.

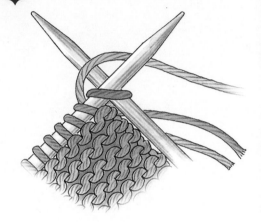

 When you're ready to change colors again, repeat steps 1 and 2. Always add your yarn on the same side of the scarf.

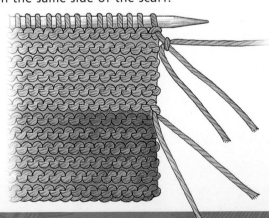

4 The row where you add the new color will look like this from the back:

5 When your scarf is complete, go back and weave all the ends into your work. Be sure to weave each end into the knitting of the same color.

fringe

If you want to add fringe at the bottom of your scarf, set aside the yarn you'll need to make it before you start knitting. That way you'll be sure to have enough. To add a 3-inch-long fringe to a 5-inch-wide scarf, you'll need about 7 yards of yarn.

1 Start by cutting a piece of yarn twice as long as you want the fringe to be. In this case we cut a 6-inch piece of yarn to make a 3-inch fringe.

2 Fold the yarn in half, then poke your crochet hook down through the last row of the scarf and pull the fringe through.

3 You'll have a loop of yarn like this:

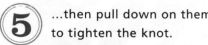

4 Pull the ends up through the loop...

5 ...then pull down on them to tighten the knot.

6 Add fringe all the way across like this, trying to space them out more-or-less evenly.

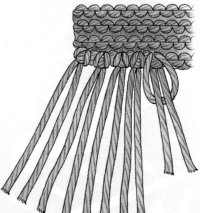

Sunglass Bag

The sunglass bag starts out with the rib stitch. This is what you usually see around the cuffs and bottom edges of your sweaters. Don't worry, it's easier than it looks.

WHAT YOU NEED
SIZE 8 NEEDLES · 40 YARDS OF WORSTED WEIGHT YARN
YOUR YARN NEEDLE

purple means knit
green means purl

30 stitches

1 Cast on 30 stitches.

2 To make the rib stitch:
Knit one stitch then **purl** one stitch. Repeat across the row. You'll end with a purl.

If you have a hard time knitting and purling in the same row, turn the page for help.

knitting and purling in the same row

The trick to knitting and purling in the same row is making sure the yarn is in the right place before each stitch.

If the next stitch loops like this... ...**knit** *next.*

Before you knit a stitch, pull the yarn around to the back of the needle as shown in the illustration.

If the next stitch goes straight across like this... ...**purl** *next.*

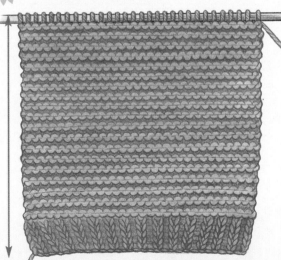

Before you purl a stitch, pull the yarn around to the front of the needle.

When you've worked the rib stitch for 1 inch, you're going to switch to the garter stitch.

To do this, **knit** all the stitches in this row...

1 inch

... then **knit** every row until your work measures 6-$\frac{1}{2}$ inches.

If you're knitting to the right gauge (see page 26), your bag will measure about 6-$\frac{1}{2}$ inches across the garter stitch section.

Cast off the next row and tie off as always.

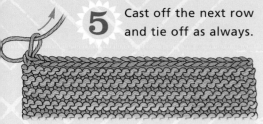

6

Fold your bag in half and sew it together along the bottom and side edge. Stop right where the ribbing starts. Weave in all your ends. You can turn the bag inside out so the seam is on the inside or, if it looks good, leave it as it is.

 Stop sewing right here.

 If you want to add a little bow, pull a 5-inch piece of yarn through the edge right where the ribbing starts. Tie the yarn into a bow, then trim the ends.

Purse

Try making this project with cotton yarn, or a cotton blend. It's not as stretchy as wool, so it will make a nice, sturdy purse. If you don't have cotton, wool or acrylic will work just fine.

WHAT YOU NEED
SIZE 8 NEEDLES · 140 YARDS OF WORSTED WEIGHT YARN · YOUR YARN NEEDLE

1 Cast on 30 stitches. **Knit** every row (this is the garter stitch)...

30 stitches

purple means knit
green means purl

2 ...until your work measures 1 inch from the top of the needle to the bottom of your work.

1 inch

Now **purl** one row.

③ Then **knit** the next.

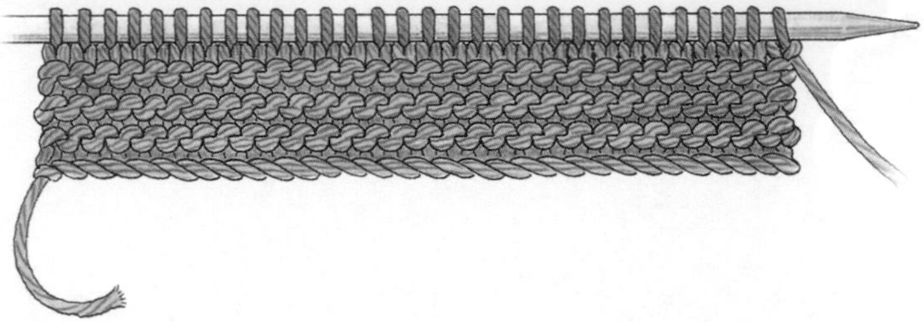

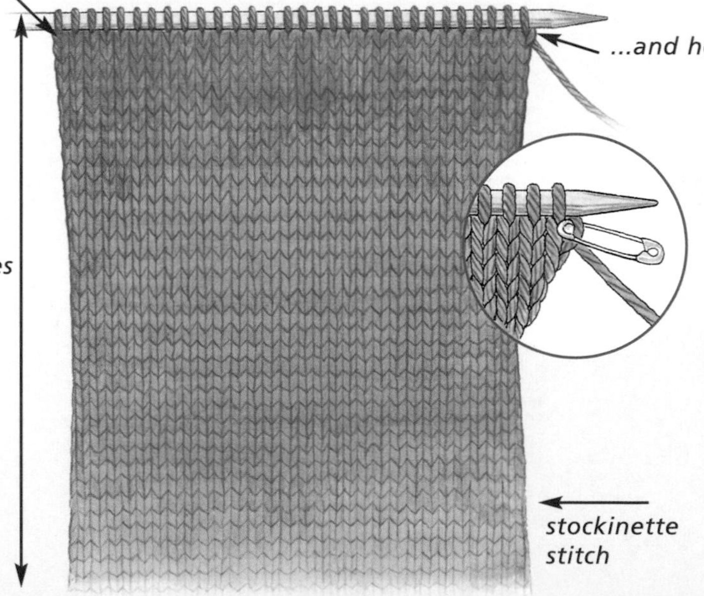

To make a purse without a flap, simply work through step 4, leaving the safety pins off. Knit 1 inch of the garter stitch (knit every row), then cast off.

④ Repeat steps 2 and 3 (**purl** one row, **knit** one row) until your purse measures 14 inches. End with a purl row even if this makes your purse slightly longer than 14 inches.

Place a safety pin on the last stitch on each side to mark this row.

Place safety pin here...

...and here.

14 inches

stockinette stitch

5 Now you're ready to start working on the purse flap. Start with a decrease row. It goes like this:

knit together · *knit together*

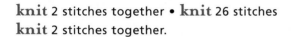

knit 2 stitches together • **knit** 26 stitches
knit 2 stitches together.

Make sure there are 28 stitches on your needle at the end of this row.

 6 Work in the stockinette stitch for three more rows:
purl one row • **knit** one row • **purl** one row

It will look like this:

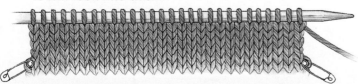

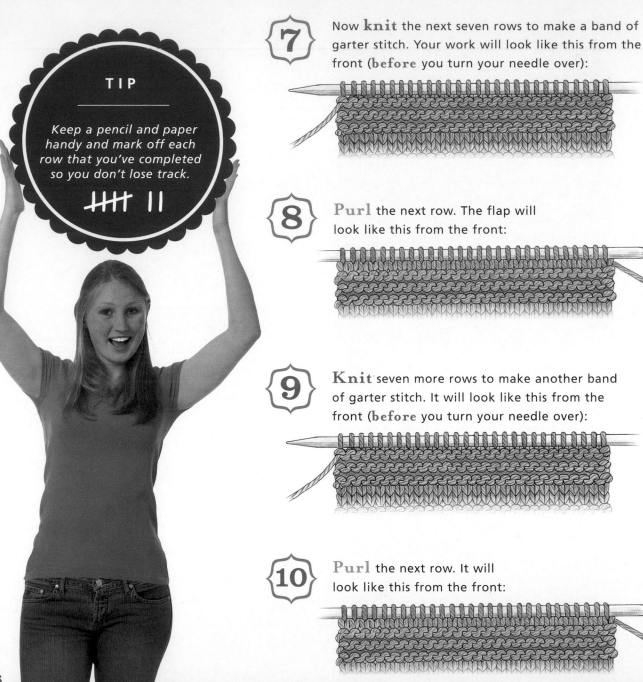

7 Now **knit** the next seven rows to make a band of garter stitch. Your work will look like this from the front (**before** you turn your needle over):

8 **Purl** the next row. The flap will look like this from the front:

9 **Knit** seven more rows to make another band of garter stitch. It will look like this from the front (**before** you turn your needle over):

10 **Purl** the next row. It will look like this from the front:

{11} **Knit** six rows to make one last band of garter stitch. It will look like this from the front:

{12}

Cast off the next row (a knit row). Tie off the end as always.

strap

The strap is made by knitting a long skinny strip of stockinette stitch. As you work, the strip will curl in on itself to make a more-or-less round cord.

1 Cast on six stitches. **Knit** across.

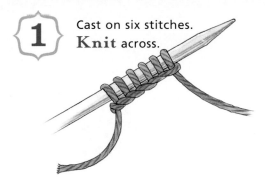

2 **Purl** the next row.

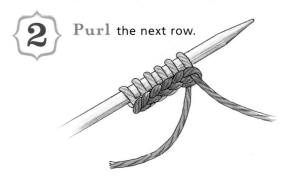

3 Repeat steps 1 and 2 until your strap is as long as you want it to be. Remember that it will stretch out a little when you start using it.

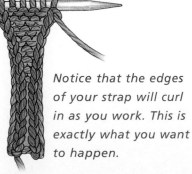

Notice that the edges of your strap will curl in as you work. This is exactly what you want to happen.

4 When the strap is as long as you want it, cast off and tie off the end.

finishing

1 Fold the bottom edge of your purse up so that it lines up with the safety pins. Make sure the right sides (the outside) of your purse face in. Sew up both sides, then turn your purse rightside out.

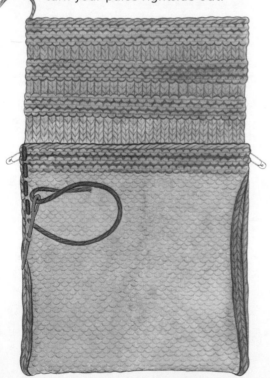

2  Using your yarn needle and some matching yarn, sew the handle securely to the inside of your purse so it sits right on top of the side seam.

3 Tie the ends together on the inside, then weave in all the ends.

Cell Phone Sock

Attach this cell sock to your purse or backpack, and you'll never have to dig through your stuff to find your phone again. This project is worked mostly in a rib stitch, and can be knit to fit your cell phone.

WHAT YOU NEED

SIZE 8 NEEDLES · 35 YARDS OF WORSTED WEIGHT YARN
A ³/₄-INCH BUTTON · YOUR YARN NEEDLE · NEEDLE AND THREAD

purple means knit
green means purl

1 Start by casting on 18 stitches.

2 For your first row, **knit** one stitch, **purl** the next. Repeat across the whole row.

TIP: If you don't know how to knit and purl in the same row, go to page 58 for help.

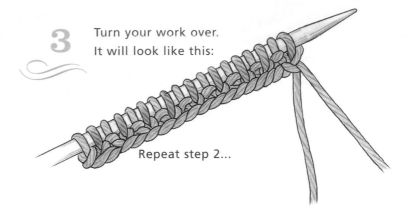

3 Turn your work over. It will look like this:

Repeat step 2...

6 Continue to alternate between a **knit** and a **purl** stitch, casting off as you go until you have only eight stitches left (one on the right needle and seven on the left). **Knit** the remaining seven stitches.

4

...until your work is twice as long as the body of your cell phone. Don't worry about the antenna.

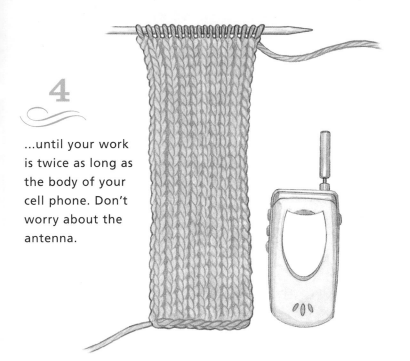

5

You'll make the handle next. To do this **knit** one stitch, **purl** the next, then cast off the first stitch by pulling it over the second stitch and off the needle.

7

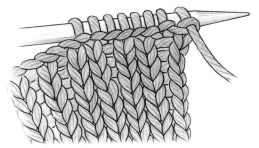

Purl all the stitches in the next row, then continue to work in the stockinette stitch (**knit** one row, **purl** the next row) until the handle measures 4 inches. End with a **purl** row (it's OK if this makes your handle slightly longer or shorter than 4 inches).

8

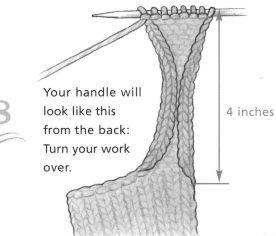

Your handle will look like this from the back: Turn your work over.

4 inches

9

Now you're going to make the buttonhole and shape the handle's end. Start by **knitting** the first two stitches.

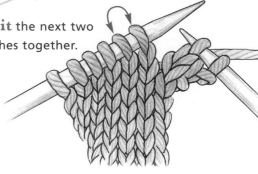

10

Knit the next two stitches together.

 = knit these
stitches together

13 ...then **knit** the two remaining stitches. Turn your work over.

11

Then wrap the yarn around the front of the right needle...

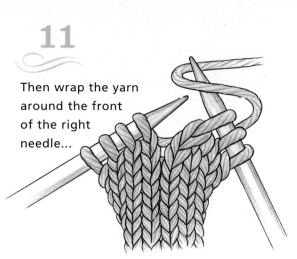

12

...so it looks like this:

Knit the next two stitches together...

14

You should have seven stitches, counting the new loop you just made.

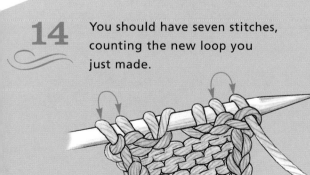

Purl the first two stitches together, **purl** three stitches (including that loop), then **purl** the last two stitches together. Turn your work over.

15

There will be five stitches on your needle.

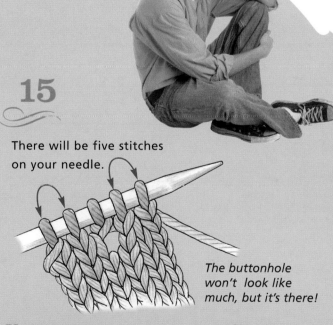

The buttonhole won't look like much, but it's there!

Knit the first two stitches together, **knit** the next stitch, then **knit** the last two stitches together. Turn your work over.

16

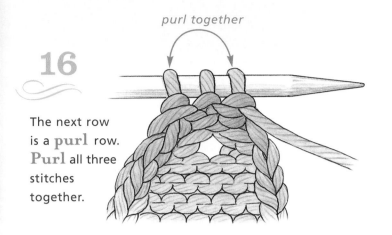

purl together

The next row
is a **purl** row.
Purl all three
stitches
together.

17

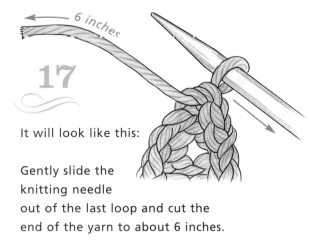

6 inches

It will look like this:

Gently slide the
knitting needle
out of the last loop and cut the
end of the yarn to about 6 inches.

18

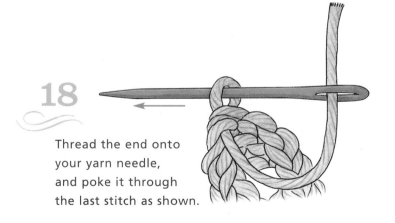

Thread the end onto
your yarn needle,
and poke it through
the last stitch as shown.

19

Pull the
knot tight.

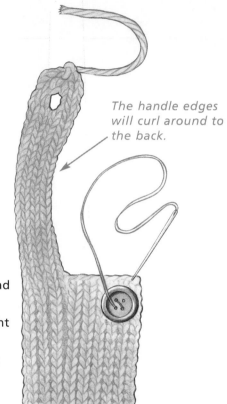

The handle edges will curl around to the back.

20

Use a regular needle and thread to sew a button onto the top right corner of the body of the sock as shown.

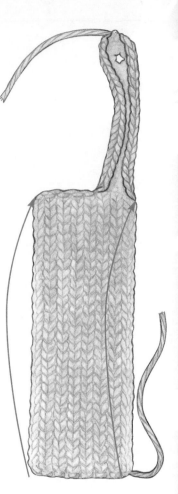

21

Turn your cell sock over and fold the bottom edge up to meet the top edge where the handle starts.

22

Use your yarn needle to sew up the two sides. If your edges are neat, you can sew on the outside without turning the sock inside-out.

When you're finished, button the cell phone sock to your purse or backpack. Perfect!

Hat

Save the hat until you've made a few of the smaller projects and feel pretty comfortable knitting. It's not hard as long as you count your stitches carefully. Really carefully.

WHAT YOU NEED

SIZE 8 NEEDLES · 130 YARDS OF WORSTED WEIGHT YARN · YOUR YARN NEEDLE

1 Cast on 84 stitches. Count them twice to be sure you've got it right. *This is important!* **Knit** the first row.

84 stitches

Your needle will be very full. Be careful that you don't let any stitches slip off the end.

purple means knit
green means purl

2 **Purl** the second row.

3 Continue to work in the stockinette stitch (knit one row, purl the next). After a few inches the bottom edge will start to roll up. This is just what you want it to do.

4 Work until your piece measures 8 inches when unrolled. End with a purl row so that your next row will be a knit row.

8 inches

Now you're ready to shape the hat. Before you start, double check to be sure you still have 84 stitches on your needle.

5 **Knit** five stitches, then **knit** the next two stitches together. Repeat across the row.

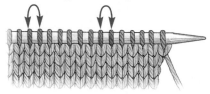

Work slowly and count carefully. You should end up with 72 stitches on your needle. If you don't, unravel the row and try again.

6 **Purl** the next row. It doesn't hurt to check again to be sure you've still got 72 stitches on the needle.

7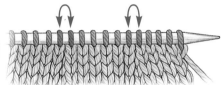

Now **knit** four stitches, then **knit** two stitches together. Repeat across the row.

You should have 60 stitches on your needle at the end of this row.

8 **Purl** the next row.

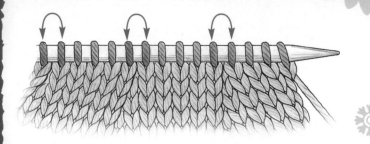

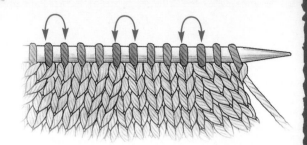

9 **Knit** three stitches, then **knit** two stitches together. Repeat across the row. *You should have 48 stitches on your needle at the end of this row.*

11 Now **knit** two stitches, then **knit** two stitches together. Repeat across the row. *You should have 36 stitches on your needle at the end of this row.*

10 **Purl** the next row.

12 **Purl** the next row.

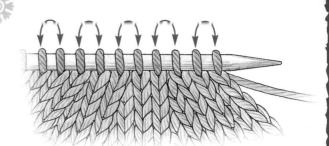

13 Knit one stitch, then knit two stitches together. Repeat across the row. *You should have 24 stitches on your needle at the end of this row.*

15 Finally, knit two stitches together across the whole row. You'll be down to 12 stitches at the end of this row.

14 Purl the next row.

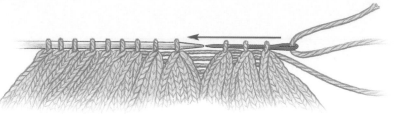

16 Finally. You're finished with all that counting. Cut the yarn so the end is about a yard long and thread it onto your yarn needle. Carefully transfer each stitch from your knitting needle to the yarn needle as shown.

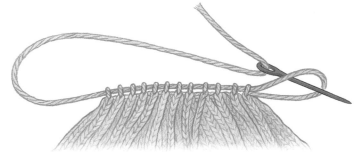

17 Pull the yarn through the stitches, leaving a little loop on the right side, then poke the yarn needle back through this loop...

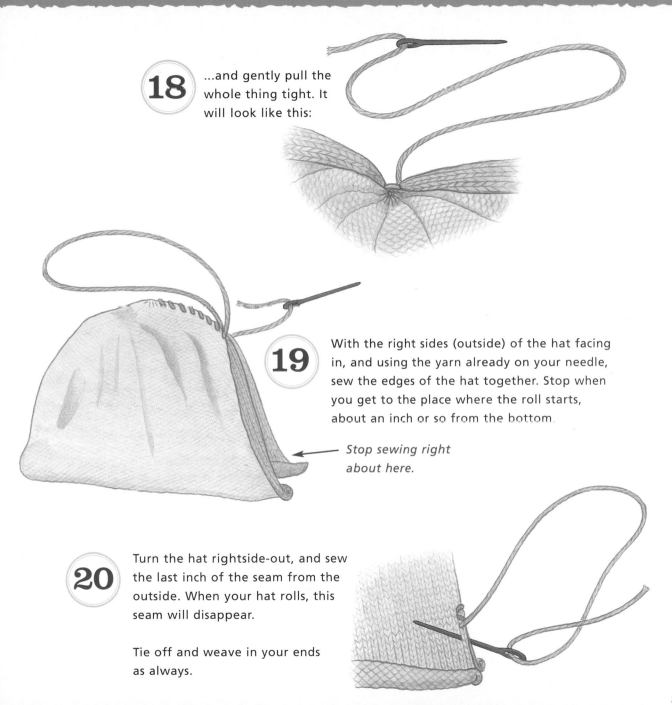

18 ...and gently pull the whole thing tight. It will look like this:

19 With the right sides (outside) of the hat facing in, and using the yarn already on your needle, sew the edges of the hat together. Stop when you get to the place where the roll starts, about an inch or so from the bottom.

Stop sewing right about here.

20 Turn the hat rightside-out, and sew the last inch of the seam from the outside. When your hat rolls, this seam will disappear.

Tie off and weave in your ends as always.

hat topper

The hat topper is made from a simple crocheted cord. To make it you'll need your crochet hook and about 4 yards of yarn. But don't cut the yarn until you're finished crocheting the cord. That way you'll be sure to have enough.

1 Start by tying a slip knot onto your crochet hook.

Leave a tail of about 6 inches.

2 Lay the long end of the yarn across your left hand so it runs behind your index finger, over your two middle fingers and behind your pinky as shown.

3 Now bring the crochet hook down so the yarn wraps around your index finger...

4 ...and pinch the short end of the yarn between your thumb and second finger to pull it taut. Good.

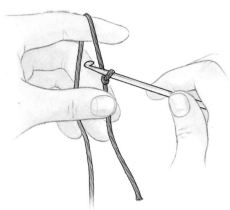

5 Use your crochet hook to pick up the yarn that runs between the slip knot and your index finger and pull it through the slip knot.

6 You've just crocheted a stitch. Repeat step 5 until you've crocheted a cord 36 inches long.

7 Cut the yarn so there's a 6-inch tail, then pull the end through the last stitch.

8 Thread your yarn needle with some matching yarn. Poke it through the first knot on your cord and a spot about 3 inches from the end.

11 Now tie the two ends of yarn together, leaving both ends about 5 inches long.

9 Continue to make loops about the same size, running your needle through them to gather them all together. The loops don't have to be exactly the same size. Close is good enough.

10 Try to make your loops so that you end with the needle running through the last stitch. If you don't get this right, back up a few loops and try again.

12 Use your needle or crochet hook to pull all four ends down into the top of the hat. Tie them together in a double knot, making sure the topper rests snugly against the hat.

thanks to everyone!

LEAD DESIGNER
Anne Schultz

DESIGNERS
Jina Choi
Efrat Rafaeli

ART DIRECTION
Jill Turney

TECHNICAL ILLUSTRATION
Valley Hennings
Darwen Hennings

PHOTOGRAPHY
Peter Fox
Richard Reader
Wendy Yalom
Angie Norwood Brown
Matt Farruggio

CALLIGRAPHY
Rosemary Woods

BUTTON DESIGN
Liz Hutnick

OUR TIRELESS KNITTERS
Rebecca Muench
Donna Swenson
Paula Hannigan
Bridget Batting
Jenny Hsin
Alice Tucker
Pat Kongsle

Special thanks to Kate Paddock, Kelly Shaffer and to all the new knitters at Klutz.

MODELS
Julie Zhu
Genevieve Yang
Dana Varinsky
Danya Taymor
Soumya Srinagesh
Lauren Slusser
Tiffanie Scott
Natalie Rosekrans
Amy Rogg
Daisy Robinton
Amber Richard
Jenni Putney
Roger Prince
Keith Putnam
Hansen Perkins
Heather Peng
Vanessa Pan
Roxana Moussavian
Emily Long
Megan Litrownik
Jessica Lee

Nicole Landau
Sara Kwasnick
Jackie Javerbaum
Morgan Holland
Annie Hodges
Shannon Harney
Ashley Gardiner
Ashley Gadson
Zoe Friesen
Jada Francois
Kaela Fox
Emily Flaxman
Melissa Da Rosa
Rachael Chiappetta
Alana Carstens
Kay Buckley
Noa Bruhis
Brittney Brown
Rina Breakstone
Sophie Ashley
Ariel Ajagu

SHOW US YOUR GENIUS!

Send us a photo of your knitted creation and it may get displayed on the Fridge of Fame at klutz.com. That's world-wide recognition! To learn more, visit klutz.com or e-mail us at thefridge@klutz.com.

• CUT OUT • FILL IN • ADD STAMP • MAIL • WAIT IMPATIENTLY

CUT OUT • FILL IN • ADD STAMP • MAIL • WAIT IMPATIENTLY

Klutz Catalog

You can order more 100% Klutz certified books from the The Klutz Catalog. It is, in all modesty, unlike any other catalog — and it's yours for the asking. Just fill in this postcard, pop on a stamp, drop it in the mail and wait impatiently for your copy to arrive.

Who are you?

Name: _____ Age: _____ ❑ Too high to count ○ Boy ○ Girl

Address: _____

City:_____ State: _____ Zip: _____

Tell us more...

What do you think of this book: _____

_____

Compliments and comments here:_____

_____

❑ Check this box if you want us to send you The Klutz Catalog.

If you're a grown-up who'd like to hear about new Klutz stuff, give us your e-mail address and we'll stay in touch.

E-mail address: _____

KNITTING

MORE GREAT BOOKS FROM **KLUTZ**

Simple Embroidery   Making Mini-Books   The Shrinky Dinks® Book
Handmade Cards   Window Art   Spool Knit Jewelry

WANT MORE?

The entire line of 100% certified Klutz products are
available online at www.klutz.com. While you're there, sign
up for our free e-newsletter, create a wish list, or
try out an activity or two.

KLUTZ®
455 Portage Avenue
Palo Alto, CA 94306

First
Class
Postage
Here